Iysobel

―――――

A Stage Play in Three Acts

by

L.L.Liggett!

14,602 words
11,107 spoken words
Flesch Reading Ease 86.5
Reading Format available.

ISBN-10: 0692601058
ISBN-13: 978-0692601051
Version A 1-30-16

Luther L. Liggett, Jr.
5053 Grassland Drive
Dublin, OH 43216

lliggett@columbus.rr.com

Table of Contents

The Players

(in order of appearance)

CHORUS.

CYRIL ORVILLA:[1]   Domicet[2] Emeritus of Almadon, brother of
                            the deceased ruler.

BROTHER CEPHAS:[3]   Priest; youngest brother of Artemis and
                            Talus; nephew of the Domicet.

TALUS ORVILL: Military Commander; brother of Artemis
                            and Cephas; nephew of the Domicet.

CHARLES CALAY: Officer serving under Talus.

ARMORER   Servant to Talus.

ARTEMIS ORVILLA: Merchant; oldest brother of Talus and
                            Cephas; nephew of the Domicet.

CORELEAY ORVILLA: Wife of Artemis.

IYSOBEL:[4]   Infant daughter of Artemis and
                            Coreleay, grand-niece of the Domicet.

THREE VILLAGERS.

SCRIBE: Servant to the Domicet.

---

[1] or-VEE-ya

[2] DOE-mee-say

[3] SEE-fass

[4] EE-soh-bell

Costumes

CYRIL, DOMICET: Full-length plain mauve robe, no belt, with a starburst brooch near his left shoulder. His long gray hair is capped with a mussed, loose fabric hat. On his right hand he wears a gold signet ring, on his feet he wears plain fabric gray slippers.

BROTHER CEPHAS: Plain floor-length robe of rough brown sack-cloth or burlap, tied at the waist with a golden cord rope, starburst brooch near his left shoulder, and sandals.

TALUS ORVILLA: Plain grey tunic, black leather belt at the waist, grey trousers sharply pressed, black boots, with a starburst brooch near his left shoulder.

CHARLES CALAY: Plain grey tunic, black leather belt at the waist, grey trousers sharply pressed, black boots, same as Talus except for brooch.

ARMORER: Partial clothing, unclean as though by intent.

ARTEMIS ORVILLA: Tunic of light green, with a starburst brooch near his left shoulder, plain trousers, no belt, gray shoes.

CORELEAY ORVILLA: Light yellow gown, a sash, a necklace of gold, and a white cap.

IYSOBEL: White gown with a cap the same as Coreleay's.

THREE VILLAGERS: Loose cape top over linen shirt, pants, sandals, hat.

SCRIBE: Loose shirt, belt, over tight pants, soft shoes.

Property List

ACT I, Scene 1: The Throne Room, Fortress Centrale

Red velvet Tapestry with a single, gold starburst, the
    family crest.
Massive uncomfortable-looking Chair with well-used padding.
Side table, with parchment scroll, deck of cards, a short
    dagger, and pen-and-ink.
One small stool at Stage Right beneath a window in the
    stone wall.
Apple for Cephas.

ACT I, Scene 2: The Armory

Large Table, several Sabers.
Grindstone.
Bass drum or tympani off-stage.

ACT I, Scene 3: The Courtyard, Merchant's Home

A desk set with a wooden chest, filled with bags of coins,
    a leather book, a pen set, papers.
A stone bench.

ACT I, Scene 4: The Armory

Ibid, Scene Two.

ACT II, Scene 1: The Throne Room

Ibid, Act I, Scene One.

Glasses of wine.

ACT II, Scene 2: Mausoleum Graveyard

Mausoleum, a columned door, the name "Orvilla" carved into
    the mantle.
Headstones in a graveyard.
Wide tree trunk, enough to hide a man.
Three bags of gold coins.
Stone next to the entrance where the gold will sit.

ACT II, Scene 3: The Throne Room

Ibid, Act I, Scene One; Banquet Table set for dinner.

ACT III, Scene 1: The Courtyard, Merchant's Home

Ibid, Act I, Scene Three.

ACT III, Scene 2: Finale, The Throne Room

Ibid, Act I, Scene One.

Spoken Word Count

	Chorus	Cyril	Cephas	Talus	Charles	Armorer	Coreleay	Artemis	Villager	Scribe	Total
ue	668										668
e	0	954	1,111	770	406	118	487	747	124	0	4,717
		954	721								1,675
				387	314	118					819
							487	747			1,234
			390	383	92				124		989
)	0	1,009	683	656	0	0	749	686	0	98	3,881
		617					253			98	968
			506	377				487			1,370
		392	177	279			496	199			1,543
	0	731	185	389	33	0	155	226	79	43	1,841
			185	180	33		155	226	79		858
		731		209						43	983
L:	668	2,694	1,979	1,815	439	118	1,391	1,659	203	141	11,10
	6%	24%	18%	16%	4%	1%	13%	15%	2%	1%	

About the Author

L.L.Liggett!

Luther L. Liggett was born March 1, 1956 to a pioneer family in Marysville, Ohio. He attended The George Washington University, graduating with a Bachelor of Arts degree in Economics with Honors, Phi Beta Kappa, then with a Juris Doctorate.

The Acorn, A Journal of the Western Sierra previously published Luther's short story, *Prairie Breeze*, El Dorado Writers' Guild, no. 34, Fall Edition, 2002, El Dorado, California.

Luther currently practices Government Relations Law in Columbus, Ohio.

Prologue

SETTING: Outside the Fortress Centrale, atop a hill
                  overlooking Almadon below.

AT RISE: Chorus stands atop the hill surveying the
                  landscape.

                        CHORUS:

    Atop a tall hill sits a stone house called
Fortress Centrale,[5] although nothing about it now
resembles a fortress: the wall and towers long
deteriorated into ruin, the elegance disguised by dis-
assembled stone scattered among numerous outbuildings
which conceal the actual residence. Yet here remains
honor: of time, of success, of unity in purpose.

    The Orvilla[6] family awoke and died for generations
in the stone house, overlooking the grain fields that
fed them all.

    As far as one might see, stalks of wheat wave in
unison, caressed by the hand of the wind. Each straw
stands straight, then bows, its seeded top heavy as
though ready to topple, only for the stalk to whip
back and then again, over and back, aligned with
thousands of neighbors swaying in the rhythm of the
breeze.

    Following the wind, a villager swings a scythe in
the same rhythm so as to catch the stalks in the sharp
curve of the blade, slicing chunks of the yellow straw
with such crispness that they fall in unison: in lined
piles to be gathered, threshed, the chaff blown away,
the straw used for bedding and for roofs, the wheat to
be eaten, or planted next season, a seasonal cycle
continued eons before and forever.

    Surrounding the fields, across the land, barren
ground shows among irregular foliage spread upon
irregular hills, as though some giant with mud on his
feet scuffed the dirt off atop the rocky landscape.

SETTING SHIFT: walking into the City.

---

[5] sen-TRAH-lay

[6] or-VEE-ya

At the foot of this tall hill sits the City-State of Almadon. Fortress Centrale remains its ruling symbol. Its current resident, aged and deteriorated as the building, embodies that honor when the need arises.

Just as any parent might protect a child, not of obligation but of paternal instinct, the Orvillas have served from feudal times as regional lords to the region as their lives' purpose, now an economic but no less vital guardianship.

The last head-of-state died recently, the widower Solaren Orvilla, Domicet of Almadon, and guardian of the government: <u>engine</u> of the economy, <u>general</u> of the military, and <u>counsel</u> to the church.

His person served as confluence for every major decision and conflict, averting civil war in politics, in business, and in personal relations. Each sphere of society flourished independently, but knew from his shadow this ever-present family continuum. Solaren held an unspoken dominion over all.

With Solaren's demise passed the concept of dominion, for advances in culture made such privilege anachronistic, the people preferring the privileges conveyed by middle-class economic freedom. And so it is today, although the people call upon Solaren's brother Cyril from time-to-time, with the honorary title of "Domicet Emeritus", he having never served in the role of Domicet officially.

SETTING SHIFT: walking among buildings.

Almadon boasts less than a hundred buildings, for a large populace never was its strength. The facilities that do exist are well-structured and efficiently maintained. Residents take pride in the history of each building, reusing the floor space for ever-changing purpose, but always preserving the façade, and the stories of transactions conducted within the walls. So a culture of contentment resides around the buildings themselves, a source of non-economic wealth unique to the land.

The lifeblood of Almadon, its strength and its power, revolves around trade: the ebb and flow of life in the province. World trade, an anomaly for such an apparent backwater, came to this unlikely crossroads as an advance-guard between distant lands and the largest centers of continental population. Other cities boasted of people, with squalor and turmoil, fires and plagues, a civil war of bacteria as well as of barons, never content to grow peacefully.

Yet Almadon grew its economy quietly, not boasting of its economic prowess. The glory of the roulette wheel belongs to the gambler, winning or losing a vast sum in a courageous, or foolhardy, spin of the wheel. But the wealth goes to the croupier: quiet, diligent, patient, taking a single coin on each transaction.

And now:

Arm outstretched, walking backward.

A ship at sea, a people afloat, their direction is free, adrift in a boat. Almadon!

CHORUS exits Stage Right.

(CURTAIN)

ACT I: TRINITY UNDONE

Scene 1: The Throne Room, Fortress Centrale

SETTING: Interior of the Throne Room, plain
                      walls of sandstone. Stage Right, a
                      stone wall with an open window,
                      daylight streaming through, a stool
                      beneath the window. Rear Stage Center,
                      upon the wall hangs a red velvet
                      tapestry with a single, gold starburst
                      at center, the family crest.

                      Stage Center stands a massive
                      uncomfortable-looking Throne with well-
                      used padding, overwhelming the room.
                      Aside the Throne left sits a side
                      table, upon which lay a parchment
                      scroll, a deck of cards, a short
                      dagger, pen-and-ink, strewn
                      haphazardly.

AT RISE: The DOMICET sits on the small stool
                      Stage Right beneath the window, chin
                      resting on his fist, thinking. Craggy
                      face, he wears a full-length plain
                      mauve robe, no belt, with a starburst
                      brooch near his left shoulder. His
                      long gray hair is capped with a mussed,
                      loose fabric hat. On his right hand he
                      wears a gold signet ring, on his feet
                      he wears plain fabric gray slippers.

                      Enter from Stage Left BROTHER CEPHAS
                      cutting an apple with a knife and
                      eating. He wears a plain floor-length
                      robe of rough brown sack-cloth or
                      burlap, tied at the waist with a golden
                      cord rope, starburst brooch near his
                      left shoulder, and sandals.

                              DOMICET

                      (tired, bored, glancing at Cephas)

        I see you found my pantry once again.
        You are most welcome, my dear nephew Cephas.
        Religion may be food for one's soul,

but the body craves an apple.

CEPHAS

Yes, my dear uncle Cyril.
A fruit of the scriptures, a fruit of life.
It tastes so sweet, and we are what we eat.
Today, this sweet taste reflects my disposition.

DOMICET

(looking away from Cephas)

Surely it is true, for Life reflects nature.
The fruit is sweetest when it is rotted.

CEPHAS

(through a mouthful of apple,
patronizing, cynical)

Thank you, Domicet, for your kindest thought.
And thank you for your ever-present home.
My dearest father, your brother Solaren,
would have approved when he sat on that Throne.

(motions to the Throne)

For the land is sweet with gold and fruit and grain,
My brother Artemis collects our share.
A piece of gold for each cart that passes through,
A cut of a crate, a slice of each pear.

My brother Talus enforces the law,
General of the armies, astride the land.
For each infraction, death the penalty.
Or for servience, peace the reward.

And you rule? In the shoes of my father?
The people seek a leader, your role or mine?
I come to talk of the future, my future,
That I may take my proper place… in this room…

DOMICET

(angry, stands)

Do not dishonor… your father!
Do not dishonor… your history!
But lay those aside:
Do not dishonor…

(pointing at the Chair)

the Office!

CEPHAS

(taken aback, recovering, solicitous)

I meant no offense, my dear Domicet.
We honor the Throne, as <u>all</u> people say.
The People's Will is an office you fit,
so upon that Throne is where you should sit!

DOMICET

(stands, walks to the Chair, touches
it)

Here indeed sat Solaren, surveyor of all,
    to rule from this perch, now lost to his fall.

This Throne…
An idle object, mere leather, metal,
paper, wood, paint, cloth, inanimate.
In water it sinks, in fire it burns,
    in air it rots, for it is just soil …

(clenches his hand, then opens as
dropping an invisible object)

Such is our whole world, my Brother Cephas!
All sprung from the soil: static, empty, dead.
Then, a life comes along!
Not animal, plant, dog or cat… but life!
Breathed into the thing,

(pauses, contemplating)

And it, too, takes on the essence of life!

It could be good, bad, handsome, ugly;
Yet now with purpose, no matter how brief,
to join the living, to play its own role.

The aggregate then, the interaction,
is who, is what we are.
Life is a dance, the motion,
of man and man-made in location.

CEPHAS

(cynical)

You, saw the Chair move?

DOMICET

No, not these many years.
But when Solaren sat there, ah, yes!
It did dance!
And the people too!

(walks back to look out the window)

They asked for Justice? The Domicet listened,
    consulted many, then righted the wrong.
They needed defense? He hired the soldiers,
    commanded respect, put fear in the foe.
They wanted a job? He worked side by side,
    shared sweat, bread, and gold, so that all
    prospered.

(facing Cephas)

I saw the Chair move! But just when he sat;
As he filled people's hearts, the Chair filled with
            life.
So I cannot sit, or fill it with life;
The man who sits there must make the Chair move.

CEPHAS

This man was mighty!

(turns aside, introspective)

Or so I am told, sent me away, then he died….

DOMICET

Back when my brother held all together,
All in one hand he ruled from that Throne.
He was their Money;
their Military;
their Justice,
their Will.

All through Almadon

(points to the window)

He was their king

(points to the Chair)

No one ever will replace my brother,
     as in the near past, the Domicet Solaren.
Like this fine mansion,

(hands upraised, laughs, shakes head)

Fortress Centrale, naught but a pile of rocks,
Now home to a lizard.
That Chair, once a Throne, now just a relic.
Now that day is gone; I am a relic.

(returns to sitting on stool, gazing
out window)

CEPHAS

(patronizing)

Among my treasured holdings are relics:
Wood of the Cross, bones of the saints, holiest oil.
The precious objects guide us through our lives.
Care for the relics, and we care for mankind.

DOMICET

(dismissive with a wave of his hand)

Ha! Dead things, idols, their former owners dead, too.
They have no value of their own.

CEPHAS

So tell me, Domicet, what do you value among your
objects?

DOMICET

(thinking; resolved, walks to the side
table, shakes a finger in the air)

I will share with you, it is limitless!
As with the air, the earth, the rain, one's life.

(picks up the scroll from the side
table, waves it)

A parchment, the writings of Cicero. Priceless!

CEPHAS

(points at the Domicet)

Thus! Our disagreement is only of choice.
You, too, revere your own priceless relic.
But that is unique, and cannot be shared;
Only one owns it, grasps it in his hand.

DOMICET

(shaking head)

Brother Cephas.
For a learned man you suffer from sin, the sin of
     ignorance.
I hold in my hand, NOTHING! Yet I own more!
It is the concept, learning I share with you;
Neither time nor space robs me of knowledge.

CEPHAS

Knowledge exists in only a fleeting life, an illusion.

(pause, venturing)

I wish to possess, to control, to live!
Of what value is Cicero except that
others pay a sum of gold for that parchment?

                    The DOMICET places the scroll on the
                    table, draws a playing card, shows it.

                              DOMICET

I draw … King of Hearts;

                    (draws again)

I draw … Ace of Spades. I turn them over,

                    (shuffles the two cards)

give one at random.

                    (hands King of Hearts to Cephas)

You turn it over, and without seeing mine,
learn by your King that my card is the Ace.

                    (each show their cards accordingly)

Now again,

                    The DOMICET takes both cards, shuffles,
                    hands one back to Cephas, both kept
                    concealed.

But, this time an angel takes you in flight!
Past the Moon gone hence at the speed of light!
Your card still unseen, you neither know mine.
But you are gone from my time and gone from my space!

                              CEPHAS

Then my knowledge means nothing, an illusion.

                              DOMICET

Now look!

                    (each shows his card)

Thus in a future time, in a different place,
you learn of your card and of mine as well.
You in the future can tell of the past;
I, in the past, can predict the future!

                    (returns card to the deck, and to the

table)

Knowledge transcends even space and time.

CEPHAS

(tosses card on the table, turns his
back to the Domicet)

Word games!
You serve me riddles when I offer honor.
That Throne is but yours, and yet you refuse to sit.
Take your place, relic or not, the world awaits!

DOMICET

I am but Cyril Orvilla, mere man.

For reason my title is Emeritus.
It is not my seat to take; only to earn.
The Wealth, the Soldiers, and most, the People's Will,
these must come together to rule on that chair.

My brother's three sons, each have a portion.
Artemis has wealth, a worthy merchant.
Talus commands the soldiers, for peace.
And the Peoples' Will,

(pauses, looks at Cephas)

has yet to find home.

(turns away)

CEPHAS

(insulted, but replying cautiously)

Men of religion depend on the gifts
of the faithful, those who love our shared truth.
So I mediate, and account for their souls;
I manage the heart; I lead them to God.

DOMICET

So you count yourself a mathematician?
Then solve this:
At the start of mankind, counting took numbers.

Name the first three sums, numbers invented.
Quite simple....

                    CEPHAS

                (carefully thinking)

Why, Zero, One, Two, of course.

                    DOMICET

A simple answer, obvious response.
Yet wrong, evidence of shallow thought.
To know this answer you must know us better.
The correct answer is Two, One, Zero.

                    CEPHAS

More word games!

                    DOMICET

                (ignoring Cephas, continues on in
                thought)

For man first to count, zero is nothing;
No one points and shouts, "Look, there is nothing!"
No, zero is nothing to counting.
Even the Romans had no zero.

As for One:

Who points to the sky, and exclaims, "Count that!
One Sun!"
It is but unique, nothing else to count.
One is dependent on another object;
One is a subset of a group of things:
not a unity, but an entity.

For counting to start, for numbers at all,
Two is the first.
And then Three, and so forth, to measure a group.
One is half of Two, a third of Three,
a quarter of Four, a fraction of all.

CEPHAS

(angered)

As with my relics, <u>your</u> purpose demeans!
What is your point with reference to <u>my</u> purpose?

DOMICET

(looks Cephas in the eyes)

You may know numbers,
      but you do not know man.

(walks away, dismissively)

CEPHAS

I know that man is driven by gold.
The merchant, he pays to each man a wage;
      and back to the merchant each man buys bread.
Threaten a man's wage, he changes his will.

DOMICET

Give him no choice, and he takes what he needs.
Careful, young Cephas;
The people choose to make things work well.
Man's will to follow cannot be compelled.

CEPHAS

Hire us a Soldier, who works with no will;
A tool of the law, of king or of gold.
A true Triangle of how each man lives;
Men buy bread, gold buys soldiers, swords keep peace!

DOMICET

Again, Brother Cephas, too simple, and so wrong!
It is each man's choice, to make the merchant wealthy.
It is each man's choice, to tolerate the soldier.
It is each man's choice, to follow a leader.

CEPHAS

You confuse politics with law!
Our people choose law!

Law must be moral.
Religion leads law.
Their hearts will follow.
This is where I lead.

(stands proud)

DOMICET

(dismissive; faces Cephas, challenging)

Arbitrary law of religious discretion.
Where does equity enter your concept?

CEPHAS

Law is equity; religion is law.
Does it not state in Deuteronomy,
"You shall appoint judges … and…
they shall judge the people with righteous judgment?"[7]

DOMICET

Such a tautology!
Law or religion, who has chosen <u>you</u>?

CEPHAS

(pauses, solicitous)

My Uncle Cyril,
Artemis has cash;
Talus commands men.
From my dead father,
what do you grant me, the third son?

DOMICET

You were the youngest; there is nothing left.
You have learning, you have religion.
The people will choose by whom they shall be led.
The matter is yet to be decided.
Now go.

Dismissing Cephas, the DOMICET returns

---

[7] Deuteronomy, Chapter 16, Verse 18, American Revised Standard Version.

> to the stool beneath the window,
> contemplates, silently ignoring Cephas.

CEPHAS

> (toward Stage Left, hesitates, an
> aside)

Does this old man not see my priestly robes?
Is he so frail to see not his power?
This country lies helpless, while he stands by.

People have no will to rule on their own.
They need wealth, power, and leaders to rule.
My father held that trinity, now split.

My brother merchant has no stomach for,
the nuances of politics and law.
But he has the wealth.

My brother soldier commands the army,
and so keeps the peace.

And without much thought, I was relegated
to a monastery for education.

Covered in these robes, I may not be king.
But I shall not be denied my birthright!
I am religion, thus I… am the law.

The People's Will bows to the soldiers' swords.
The soldiers shall march as I do direct,
paid by the coin of my rich brother.

Now, only to deal with his wife and his child.

> CEPHAS starts to exit Stage Left,
> stops, turns back with a thought.

Three rivers unite, to turn out so well;
the confluence be, the child, … Iysobel!

> CEPHAS exits Stage Left.

(CURTAIN)

ACT I: TRINITY UNDONE

Scene 2: The Armory

SETTING: Interior of The Armory, grey stone
                        walls, unadorned, not well-lit, with a
                        few small grated windows. Stage Center
                        is a large table with several sabers.

AT RISE: ARMORER stands behind the table with a
                        grindstone in hand, sharpening each
                        saber. He is an ugly brute, wearing
                        partial clothing, unclean as though by
                        intent. Yet the Armorer is of a benign
                        demeanor, slobbering uncontrollably,
                        uncouth by lack of others' care or
                        disability through no fault of his own.

                        Stage Left, CHARLES CALAY, Military
                        Officer, dressed in plain grey tunic,
                        black leather belt at the waist, grey
                        trousers sharply pressed, black boots.
                        The Officer slashes with a saber at an
                        imaginary enemy, practicing and
                        stretching.

                        Enter from Stage Right TALUS ORVILLA,
                        dressed similarly to the Officer in
                        plain grey tunic, black leather belt at
                        the waist, grey trousers sharply
                        pressed, black boots, with a starburst
                        brooch near his left shoulder.

                           TALUS

                        (casual, friendly; ignores Armorer,
                        waves grandly)

Charles Calay!
The slash of your saber vibrates the air,
    as might scare a foe from merely the wind!

                           CHARLES

Commander Orvilla! Talus!

                        (pauses to rest)

    It is I who is scared of the young cadets,

who see promotion in bettering me.
But I surprise them with many tactics;
For youth use raw strength, when tact would serve them
best.

                    TALUS

                (laughing)

And what about elders, who know all <u>your</u> tricks?

                    (picks up a saber from the table,
                    brandishes it)

                    CHARLES

                    (ignores Talus, stretching in a
                    swordsman's stance)

You posture as though working up to bet!
You keep your money; instead, I shall take your pride!

                    TALUS

Ah! Pride of Achievement, blazoned on your breast!
Some soldier's medal, or maybe a scar?
That is tradition in the soldier's world.

                    (contemplative, looking at the sword
                    blade.)

We place great value on but a fleshy coin.

                    CHARLES

Maybe the gold is good for the widow,
but, it serves no purpose in a soldier's purse.
Better to trade the medal for a tale!
In retirement, a soldier is wealthy when someone
listens.

                    TALUS

                (introspective)

In a soldier's life, tales are mother's milk.
Little more awaits. Death is his father.
But I, as commander, earn a legacy,
of power, and terror, and glory, over all.

CHARLES

You have earned much more. Now sit back and reign.

TALUS

(scornful)

The front is my place! Never forget that.

(raises his saber to challenge in a duel)

CHARLES

Commander, Talus,

(hesitates)

Swordsmen are plenty, we need not your arm.
But your leadership we cannot replace.
Risk no needless cut; I concede!

(bows)

TALUS

I do thank you, Charles, for your warm concern.
But, avoiding a fight is not my nature.

TALUS strikes at CHARLES, who raises his saber in defense just in time, as the sabers clash once. Slowly they begin a saber drill, gently touching sabers, CHARLES thrusting gently back, TALUS parrying in defense, then the reverse right-of-way, slowly at first and then more rapidly as in a practice drill.

Offstage, sound over of military drums, drumroll, then single bass drum beat.

TALUS and CHARLES stop to listen.

CHARLES

Ah, an execution!

TALUS

The peace be with us.

ARMORER

(arms outstretched)

"Woe to the bloody city, all full of lies and booty -
     no end to the plunder!
The crack of whip, and rumble of wheel, galloping
     horse and bounding chariot!
Horsemen charging, flashing sword and glittering
     spear, hosts of slain, heaps of corpses,
Dead bodies without end - they stumble over the
     bodies!"

               TALUS, CHARLES stop the drill, stare at
               the Armorer, questioning by their eyes
               the interruption.

ARMORER

(smiles for approval)

Book of Nahum, Chapter 3, Verse 1.

               (nods head, smiles, goes back to work
               sharpening sabers)

CHARLES

(head shake)

I do not think he minds us.

TALUS

I do not think he has a mind!

               Each take their stance to drill, each
               cautiously waiting for the other to
               begin.

CHARLES

Many are talking that dear Artemis
refuses the coin to fund your campaign.

        (thrusts hard in a lunge at Talus, who
        parries, pauses)

TALUS

What is true is true, and what is said is of no value.

        (thrusts at Charles, who parries)

I tell you this now: While we keep the peace,
business does profit.

        (Charles   thrusts   at   Talus,   who
        parries.)

Thus I shall be paid, willing or taken.

(thrusts at Charles, who parries)

CHARLES

Earned and should be paid, I agree with you.
But, never break the peace, or we all shall be poor!

        (thrusts at Talus, who parries)

TALUS

That is a soft and simple sentiment.
I shall recall it when I count my gold.

        (thrusts at Charles, who parries)

CHARLES

Careful, commander!

        (backing up against a wall, worried
        about receiving an injury)

Do not risk folly!

        (thrusts at Talus, who parries)

                         TALUS

                 (taking advantage, fighting harder in
                 slow but deliberate slashes)

Open eyes must see, let them oppose me,
and a multitude shall pay with their lives!

                 (thrusts at Charles, who parries)

                 Offstage, sound over of military drums,
                 drumroll, then single bass drum beat.

                 TALUS and CHARLES stop to listen.

                         ARMORER

                 (arms outstretched)

"Their flesh shall rot while they are still on their
feet, their eyes shall rot in their sockets, and their
tongues shall rot in their mouths!"

                 (chuckles to self, goes back to work)

                         ARMORER

                 (looks up, serious, authoritative)

Zechariah, Chapter 14, Verse 12.

                         CHARLES

                 (laughing)

His tongue does spit out of turn!

                         TALUS

                 (angry)

His tongue shall turn on a spit!

                 Each take their stance to restart the
                 drill.

                         CHARLES

Soldiers you command, but not people's hearts.
And do not forget, your purse is empty.

(thrusts at Talus, who parries)

TALUS

The gold I shall take, when a brother dies….

(thrusts at Charles, who parries)

CHARLES

(stops the drill)

You cannot mean that!

TALUS

I do!
For the politics, for the People's Will,
they shall have no choice…

CHARLES

Do not dare say it!

TALUS

(quickly finishing the thought)

…but to embrace me!

I have an ally, truly a black knave!
He'll bring them to me, if I share the chair.
I share, to a point. For my point…

(points saber in the air)

… they fear!

CHARLES

(cautioning)

You do challenge Fate, and risk the People,
To share and share alike with a traitor.
Whether at a point, or by a gallows' rope:
Unite against them, and it's Death you will share.

                        TALUS

Fate?

                    (stabs   at   Charles,   who   surprised,
                    parries just in time, clashing sabers)

Fate?

                    (stabs at Charles, who parries)

No ghost guides my hand,
nor writes my record!
I ...

                    (angrily   slashes   at   Charles,   who
                    parries)

am ...

                    (slashes   once   again   at   Charles,   who
                    parries, backs up)

my ...

                    (slashes   again   at   Charles,   who parries,
                    backs up)

own ...

                    (slashes   again   at   Charles,   who parries
                    and falls)

   fate!

                    (slashes   hard   at   Charles,   who   barely
                    misses injury)

                    Offstage, sound over of military drums,
                    drumroll, then single bass drum beat.

                    TALUS and CHARLES stop to listen.

ARMORER

(arms outstretched)

Eat your own, Kill your kin,
never look you back!
Hear them moan, Bear your sin,
pain, you'll never lack!

TALUS, CHARLES look at the Armorer for
an explanation.

ARMORER

(serious,   slowly,   head   down,
embarrassed)

Uh, it's a prophecy. I made that up.

CHARLES

(forced laugh to Talus, nodding at the
Armorer)

I see our future in death…

TALUS

I see his death in our future!

TALUS and CHARLES resume a friendly
drill. As the two begin, the ARMORER
is curious, and moves in front of the
table to stand behind Talus, moving
with each move, mimicking Talus,
watching intently. TALUS and CHARLES
start slowly, then evenly accelerate as
to an accelerating metronome.

TALUS

It is our trade, Charles, that others must die;
a deadly business, but merely a business!

(Talus slashes once at Charles, who
parries)

CHARLES

(taunting)

You, a master tradesman,
me, a novice apprentice?
A full purse in hand,
I shall strut, no doubt?

(Charles slashes, Talus parries)

TALUS

You mock me, my friend; serious I am!

(Talus slashes at Charles, who parries)

CHARLES

A mock it is not, if more than a purse!

(Charles slashes at Talus, who parries)

TALUS

So, cash is not master? Luxury indeed!

(Talus slashes at Charles, who parries)

CHARLES

I have my needs, true, but, duty still rules me.

(Charles slashes at Talus, who parries)

TALUS

Ha! You deceive yourself, and now lie to me!

(Talus slashes at Charles, who parries)

CHARLES

(angry)

Never you question my loyalty to you!

(Charles slashes at Talus, who parries)

                    TALUS

                        (testing)

You'll kill at my word?

                    (Talus slashes at Charles, who parries)

                    CHARLES

I'll do my duty.

                    (Charles slashes at Talus, who parries)

                    TALUS

Your life is my own?

                    (Talus slashes at Charles, who parries)

                    CHARLES

My life is MY own!

                    (Charles slashes at Talus, who parries)

                    TALUS

Then pledge me your soul!

                    (Talus slashes at Charles, who parries)

                    CHARLES

I pledge you my sword!

                    (Charles slashes at Talus, who parries)

                    TALUS

Not enough!

                    (Talus slashes at Charles, who parries)

                    CHARLES

All you get!

                    (Charles slashes at Talus, who parries)

TALUS

You die!

(Talus slashes at Charles, who parries)

CHARLES

I live!

(Charles slashes at Talus, who parries)

TALUS

NO!

TALUS slashes with fury at CHARLES, who tries to parry, but drops his saber. From the force CHARLES falls backward, balancing himself on his hands to escape. TALUS charges with outstretched arm, points and holds his saber at Charles' throat, while calming down.

TALUS

You are my true friend, a soldier in arms.
NEVER doubt my word, my promise to you!
In my time, I shall rule, kindly or, deathly cruel.
Your choice: office high; now join me - or die!

CHARLES

You need only ask.

TALUS

The time will come….

CHARLES

Your brother?

TALUS

Of course.

CHARLES

And Iysobel?

                         TALUS

My dilemma.

                    Talus waits until CHARLES slowly nods
                    his assent.

                    The ARMORER standing directly behind,
                    TALUS with arm straight and extended,
                    whirls the saber in a single sweep
                    behind, striking the Armorer in the
                    neck in a single, fatal blow.

                    Stage dark.

                    The ARMORER screams in agony, a thud as
                    he slumps to the floor dead.

                    (CURTAIN)

ACT I: TRINITY UNDONE

Scene 3:   The Courtyard, Merchant's Home

SETTING: The Courtyard of the Merchant's home is
                            bright and open, a low stone wall
                            lining Rear Stage Center, entangling
                            vines meandering along the stone, a
                            tree behind the wall. Front center, a
                            stone bench. Stage Right is a desk
                            upon which is a wooden chest, a leather
                            book, a pen set, and papers.

AT RISE: ARTEMIS the Merchant is dressed in a
                            tunic of light green, with a starburst
                            brooch near his left shoulder, plain
                            trousers, no belt, gray shoes.

                            CORELEAY, his wife, is dressed in a
                            light yellow gown, a sash, a necklace
                            of gold, and a white cap.

                            Artemis and Coreleay sit back-to-back
                            upon the stone bench.

                            IYSOBEL, dressed in a white gown with a
                            cap the same as her mother's, sits on
                            her mother's lap.

                            CORELEAY

                   (cooing, sing-song, to the child)

   The sun is bright yellow, The moon is bright white;
   I love this young fellow, His love is my might.
   And you, my small child, Our love's evidence.
   Your lifetime so mild, Our true Recompense.

                            ARTEMIS

                (philosophically talking to the air)

   Iysobel my child, are you now happy?
   Sitting on her lap, wrapped in mother Coreleay's arms?
   The world around us in struggle and strife.
   How will you survive when we depart life?

                            CORELEAY

(angered, covers the child's ears)

Here now, Artemis! You'll frighten the child!
Do not speak to her of your workday world.

ARTEMIS

And yet, Coreleay,
you would have her reign, one day as a queen?
The sooner then that she knows the world's truth!
Money or hunger, warring or the threat,
disease, aging, theft, what shall we spare her?

CORELEAY

Must you always stay at the same, sad place?
You are so wealthy, and the eldest heir.

CORELEAY places Iysobel on the floor,
stands, looks at Artemis.

Take hold the reins, sit in the chair and reign!
It is yours to rule, why do you run?

ARTEMIS

(disinterested)

Ah! Is it that again? You want me to govern?
To sit on a throne, to be choked by people?
To pretend that I listen, and that I love them?
To greet and wave, all an empty gesture?

CORELEAY

Yes! Of all three brothers you are to follow;
but your father's chair now sits empty of all.
It is first their loss, and second your loss.
Face your duty, embrace your future!

ARTEMIS

My uncle Cyril, Domicet now,
he can hold the chair, await a better heir.
I have no interest in power, in fame.
Just business, the business of our nation.

CORELEAY

And, ignore my wishes to bargain the same?

                    ARTEMIS

            (jumps   up,   turns   around   to   face
            Coreleay)

Ah! The fish sinks the bobber!

                    CORELEAY

            (petulant)

No, no, that's not what I meant. It is…
It is… that you <u>deserve</u> to govern, to rule.
Cephas is a priest, no money, no soldiers;
And you must not leave the Throne to deathly Talus!

                    ARTEMIS

            (disinterested again, sits)

Talus is my brother, father's second son.
He holds together the country today.
Cephas has his role, comforting people,
Third son, still family, we need him too.

                    CORELEAY

To what future?
Of sword, blood, famine and threat?
Of fear, war, disease and death?
Where will be <u>my</u> place?

                    Catching   herself,   CORELEAY   looks
                    furtively around, and runs to Iysobel.

Where is Iysobel's place?

                    ARTEMIS

Talus has no interest in you. But… the child?
He needs the money, he wants the power.
Secure those things, you, the child will be safe.
In my gold, in his greed, is your haven.

                    (sits back, resigned to work on papers)

                    CORELEAY

(anger boils over)

You selfish, selfish man!

ARTEMIS

(stands, ignores her, walks to the desk)

The papers pile up; I must see to my books.

CORELEAY

(cools, tries different tack, seats child on the bench)

I brought you a child, now seek my own future.
My past is royal, my present is loyal,
My future should be fair, a place among us.
What shall be my work? What of my talent?

ARTEMIS

Talent? Talent?
It was the talents of your silver dowry
That gained the glance of my father.

(opens the chest, takes out a bag of coins, shakes the bag)

It is Money you have; do not confuse the two.

(tosses the bag to land on the floor in front of Coreleay)

CORELEAY

(cynically self-deprecating)

Ah, yes.
A captive, the spouse, just philanthropist,
a tool for the man.
My dowry expands, first a child, then land;
Exhibitionist to wear fancy clothes.
Paid for as wages to a common slave.
Do I add nothing?

CORELEAY circles toward desk, smiling, swishing her skirt until she has

Artemis's attention.

Ignorant, blind man!
To this house I bring: Art to rest your eyes,
Music that we sing; Beauty of my own.
Culture in my speech, Interest in your work,
Knowledge that I teach; And above all,

Love;

> (points to Iysobel)

A Mother's Love for her.

> (points to Artemis)

Wifely Love for you;

> (pointing outside)

Queenly Love for them!

And for all of that I shall not take pay,
but claim ownership equal to your share.
What you earn, I too. If you spend, I too.
If you rule, I too. It is mine, by… right.

ARTEMIS

> (exasperated, sits back)

Then it is all yours; please take it from me;
For then you shall find that I own nothing.

> (pauses, stands, pays sincere attention
> to Coreleay)

And you are so right, to claim what I have.
For the gifts you bring earn much more than cash.
It is a tight trap!

Each time I savor your earthly presence, I am torn in
    two:
Heaven to please you, Hell to disappoint!
And what do I gain for making the choice?

> ARTEMIS taunts with a pause, CORELEAY
> wondering whether he is pleased or

angry, then smiles.

I confess … my Love! That is my reward!

Each morn I awake and seek your being,
and then take my rest, for all is secure.
For there is no Art but your lithe body,
not marble but real flesh, arresting my gaze.

And, Music is your voice, wafting on the air.
Your Beauty coaxes fragrance from flowers;
Your Culture of speech mingles in my ear;
I savor the sound while begging for more.

I am flattered by your Interest in my work;
And I learn from your Knowledge of this world.

Truly that <u>is</u> Love!
Not partner but <u>part</u> of my very essence,
my being, my soul.

Do not doubt my deed,
that all I have is yours to own alone.
For I own nothing but,
my Love for you.

(waits for her reaction)

CORELEAY

(curtsies)

You, are too kind, sir.
A lover fears loss when often ignored and not
    reminded.

(calmly returns to the bench and child)

ARTEMIS

(sits back down at desk)

Now I must return to dreary duty,
the economics of reality.
I run a business: trade something away,
trade something back, and pay in the course.

ARTEMIS, contemplative, picks out one

                              gold coin out of the chest, and holds
                              it up to examine.

One gold Solaren, named for my father,
like the sun shining, a radiant orb.
Money is the grease, to gain our purpose.
Gold without a goal is useless metal.

This chest of gold coin belongs to people,
who make bread and wine, or serve as soldiers.
Their daily living makes society.
We hold gold in trust, to motivate them.

                    ARTEMIS pulls five bags of gold out of
                    the chest.

One bag for the mill;
One for the tailor;
Three for my brother,
Talus the soldier.

                         CORELEAY

Three!

Why so generous, to a man who waits
only for your death that he gains the Throne?
Three! That he pays soldiers to build his power,
to plan and to plot, to seek your demise.

                         ARTEMIS

                    (chuckles)

Fear not dear Talus, his methods are overt;
All that he acts on is done in a day.
It is his path we avoid, his desire;
Striking out only at those in his way.

If my brother Talus wants, he'll just kill me.

                    (contemplative)

No, that is not the problem.
Fear the Brother who thinks!
Ah… There is the danger!

                    (returns to counting coins)

CORELEAY

They are your brothers!
Joined at your mother's breast,
Raised at your father's knee,
Why should you fear them?

ARTEMIS

Each man has his price.
Talus wants money;
Cephas wants power;
I just want life.

I'll not tempt either;
To each I shall give
all they desire.
Then we shall be safe.

CORELEAY

Does the Domicet Cyril not share in your wealth?

ARTEMIS

(thoughtlessly looking through papers)

He suffers no need; Neither is he heir,
as are my brothers, as to my father.
It is I who should ask what I inherit.
More than just money, or the curse to rule.

CORELEAY

And what of our child?

ARTEMIS

She shall be safe, too.
Greed causes blindness. Power pulls toward one goal.
Avoid the two, no heat will fire their passions.
With no money, with no power, no one shall touch her.

CORELEAY

(furious)

Traitor! Coward! Thief!
Betray her birthright,
Run from her defense,
Steal her future!

ARTEMIS

(slams fist on the desk)

It is decided!
I'll not risk the girl be corrupted by deathly power!
Her life is precious, more so than my own;
Power is vacant of value or worth.

(pauses, calms down)

Let them send armies,
let them waste gold
for that Throne.
I shall not yield….

(sits, head in hands)

Stunned, CORELEAY turns and casually
walks to the bag of gold on the floor,
picks it up.

CORELEAY

Ere you lose the Throne, you shall gain a fight,
to walk away or to hand it elsewhere.
Count your assets, friend: to take on this task,
you will need me, and …

CORELEAY opens the bag of gold, reaches
in for a handful of coins, throws them
at Artemis.

ALL of your money!

CORELEAY drops the bag, picks up
IYSOBEL, and marches off Stage Left.

(CURTAIN)

ACT I: TRINITY UNDONE

Scene 4: The Armory

SETTING: Ibid, Scene Two.

AT RISE: Stage Center, TALUS and CHARLES CALAY
                            sit talking, propped against the table,
                            swords in hand. Enter Cephas casually
                            swaggering, as though owning the place.

                            TALUS

Hello?
My brother Cephas; you were not announced.
You must want something; what else could bring you?

                            CHARLES

Perhaps a mission, or a tasteless chore?
Hope unrequited, a political whore?

                            CEPHAS

                    (abstractedly)

Ah, a linear mind!
Rational, logical, simple,
all in place to understand.
But, no place emotion!

                            TALUS

                    (chuckles, points sword at Cephas)

You may be artful, but you hide nothing….

                            CEPHAS

Out of your own fear you look for shadows.
Finding none, you crouch,

                    (like a tiger, knees bent, fingers at claws)

ready to pounce on anything that nears,
whether friend or foe!

TALUS

Survival is blunt. But alive we stay,
with the loss of an occasional friend.
It is that talent through which I live,
And to the grave the enemy send.

CEPHAS

(relaxes, laughs, shrugs)

Well, I am your brother, not some foreign fiend.
I will trust you, and you will not kill me….

TALUS

No, it never came to mind.

Trumpet in the background; Talus rises
from sitting on table and walks.

TALUS

Though my time is not free, your timing is good.
We expect guests, villagers with some business.

Enter Stage Left, three VILLAGERS, each
wearing loose cape top over linen
shirt, pants, sandals, hat.

TALUS

Welcome, citizens!
I am Talus, son of Solaren, commander of the military
        forces.
And this is Charles Calay, my officer.
And of course, you know my brother, your Brother
        Cephas.

CEPHAS

In the name of our Lord, welcome all.

(opens his arms)

VILLAGER ONE

Commander Talus, Brother Cephas,

>   (removes hat, bows, fidgeting)

we come to present our account, to …

                         VILLAGER TWO

>   (removes hat, bows, fidgeting)

To ask for some justice, at least a little, to …

                         VILLAGER THREE

>   (hat on, points outside)

We delivered grain to the church,
cattle to its larder,
and got nothing for the effort.
We want paid.

                         CEPHAS

Is it not enough to serve your clergy?

                         VILLAGER ONE

A good point, a fair point…

                         VILLAGER TWO

Yes, like the point on that sword!

>   (points to Talus)

                         VILLAGER THREE

We serve bread, we serve meat.
But without pay, we'd gladly serve clergy!

                         CEPHAS

Pray, a concession? Let the church work out a service
in-kind.

                         VILLAGER ONE

A special prayer!

VILLAGER TWO

A free wedding!

VILLAGER THREE

A team of priests to pull my plow, to milk my cow?

CEPHAS

(dismissive)

Consider it a tithe!
You have done God's work, you receive God's blessing.
"Blessed are the poor, for they shall receive the
kingdom of heaven!"

VILLAGER ONE

(nodding in agreement)

"The meek shall inherit the earth!"

VILLAGER TWO

(nodding in agreement)

"They who hunger and thirst for righteousness shall be
satisfied!"

VILLAGER THREE

Surely you meant, "Blessed are the poor in <u>spirit</u>."
In <u>this</u> kingdom, with nothing but spirit,
we'll go from poor to dead!

TALUS

Please, please, Brother Cephas, my friends.
Consider the payment to be my privilege.
My brother Artemis to me gives or lends,

              (picks of bag of gold from table, hands
              it to Villager 3)

Now return in peace.

              VILLAGERS bow, exit Stage Left.

CEPHAS

A waste of coin to settle their purpose.

TALUS

And there is purpose in your coming here;
I know my brother Cephas.

CEPHAS

(pauses)

Life…is truly "Art".
As intellect grows, "Art" must become our highest
achievement.
I am an "Art"-ist! In brown, barren robes.
I eat from the hand of my family,
blessed they who are wealthy, free to pursue… "Art".

TALUS

You speak in riddles. Do not confuse me now.

CEPHAS

But, my palette is not paint, or clay, or song;
My medium is… humanity's soul!
So I paint, I mold, I caress each man,
that his potential blossoms as he grows.

And all together, the community, is
a master work, or a complex quilt,
a gallery full of successful people.
That then is my Art!

I cannot account to a rational standard.
I cannot measure by the count of souls.
It is only by the eye that we judge success.
And I have come today… to enlist your help,

CHARLES

At last, here it comes!

CEPHAS

>   (ignores the comment, but just keeps
>   going)

The People, the Power, the Money, the Might,
From discord to question, determined land.
To win from their heart, the wealth and the right,
I ask, my dear brother, your sword, and your hand.

TALUS

And I, no mind? No title, no land, no…money?

CEPHAS

In people I am wealthy. In purse I am not.

TALUS

Yet Art do you claim; so I claim my Art too!
The Art of death, and destruction, deep blood red;
A landscape drenched, that all eyes comprehend,
Futility to resist, inevitable.

No wealth, no power, no people, spiritless,
Yet I alone the future command.
That is the power of the sword, not of the pen.
Together we work, for me, I demand.

>   (points at Cephas to emphasize)

Your choice.

CEPHAS

You win! I concede!

>   (hands in the air, surrenders)

And how long do you live?
Your momentous victory but a moment.
Without coin, without control, without their hearts.
You lose! Your power is sand in the wind!

CHARLES

He'll take his chances; and the land!

>   (chuckles to himself, self-confident,
>   turns away)

CEPHAS

And yet, we might have it all, with us beside,
To combine our talents, our powers, with sums
of money, our brother at our command!
This my goal, will you join?

TALUS

>   (contemplating)

If your plan works, it is noble;
If your plan fails, we are traitors.
How can I tie you to my chance, lest the loss,
That your future either is my life or death?

CEPHAS

>   (pulls off his gold rope belt, and
>   offers it to Talus)

This I give as my bond. All will know its name,
That I am tied to your fortune, ours is one.
And thus power, and money, and heart the same,
As in our father, united, we are done.

>   TALUS takes the rope belt; each embrace
>   the other in their arms.

>   CEPHAS exits Stage Left.

CHARLES

A sign? A talisman? Do you trust him?

TALUS

No, he thinks too much.

>   (paces, thinking)

A rope that binds, but two brothers or three?
And who at the hind, who at the lead?
Cephas has nothing, Artemis has all.
I will enquire, and then I shall call.

CHARLES

I am at your service!

(bows)

TALUS

I would do it myself, but likely accused.
A surrogate plan would move fate along.
In the event Artemis fails to agree,
I would ask you to see that he be gone.

CHARLES

An unpleasant task, but reality requires
we accept the only door left open.
Today we just equivocate, adrift;
So now resolve, and we anchor our fate.

TALUS

You would do this?

CHARLES

Just tell me so.

TALUS

Truly you are my comrade in arms!

The two embrace in agreement.

CHARLES

And I shall be your general in arms once done!

Both laugh.

TALUS:

Only one issue remains…

CHARLES

Yes, the issue of Artemis and Coreleay.
Shall I count that my duty as well?

TALUS

No, no.
To be the leader, I must rise alone,
That last act shall consecrate all as my realm.
A sinner no more, to the state I atone,
Then sit on the Throne, to stand at the helm!

(CURTAIN)

ACT II: UNIFICATION

Scene 1: The Throne Room, Fortress Centrale

SETTING: Ibid, Act I, Scene One.

AT RISE: Stage Right, the DOMICET sits on his
                            stool looking out the window, wine
                            glass in hand.

                            Stage Left, SCRIBE dressed in loose
                            shirt, belt, over tight pants, soft
                            shoes, stands with wine bottle and
                            second glass half full.

                            Enter CORELEAY from Stage Left,
                            carrying IYSOBEL, takes wine glass from
                            Scribe, stops Stage Center.

                         CORELEAY

                    (raises glass to Cyril)

Good day, Domicet!

                    (to Iysobel)

Say "Good Day, Uncle Cyril!"

                            CORELEAY puts IYSOBEL down, who says
                            nothing, instead runs off Stage Left;
                            SCRIBE confused, chases IYSOBEL off
                            Stage Left.

                         DOMICET

                    (laughs)

My little "Izabella"! She has better sense than to
stay with an old man!

                         CORELEAY

Not old, but mature as a fine wine;
Not foolish, but wise as the great owl;
Not weak, but strong as the tempered blade!
Not blind, but all-knowing as the sun in the sky.

DOMICET

You patronize me but,
I shall bask in your honors.

(toasts Coreleay)

CORELEAY

(coyly)

And such is the honor:
Your hand shall anoint, the next, and the next…

DOMICET

Ah! Such is my thought:
In time, and in time…

CORELEAY

(abruptly changes subjects, offers a
toast)

To… the education of Iysobel!

DOMICET:

To Izabella!

(both toast)

CORELEAY

My dear uncle, twice you are mistaken!
A minor slip, I admit, but it is her name.

DOMICET

Do you think I'm too old not to know my words?
Well-chosen they are, for to name our future.
The sound shall inspire for all who heard;
All in her name.

An "Izabella" is wise

(drawn out, "wiize")

a leader in trade.

The "bella" means war, a cloud in the distance,
unmistakably there, but to call upon,
a leader of soldiers.
Or, the "bella" means chimes, a joy to her people.
The one who will win their hearts.

                    CORELEAY

We spoke of her education, not her reputation.

                    DOMICET

Yet her reputation follows her learning.

She must learn of money, so to govern men.
She must learn of battle, so to prevail in war.
She must learn of the heart, so to brighten our world.
All of this for the child, there is no time to waste!

Izabella!

                    CORELEAY

                    (angered)

For shame! You talk of her future, yet she is a
     child!
Where is the time for play, for dolls, for song and
     for dance?
In the name of her future, you rob her of the present!
I will not have it!

                    DOMICET

Waste precious time, yet demand her a destiny?

                    (quietly)

For play she shall bargain, for silk and for treasure.
For dolls, she'll have soldiers, to march on command.
For song and for dance, she'll live among people.
For ever, her rule will be revered,
A Golden Era!

CORELEAY

(appalled)

For dolls she'll have soldiers?

DOMICET

That is her destiny, or… an early grave.

CORELEAY

(turns and paces)

She shall know wealth, not needy nor poor.
She shall be safe, sheltered from blood and sin.
She shall have grace, in words and in deed.
She shall have beauty, both outside and in.
Never to work, never to bleed, never to preach, a
vision on the hill!

DOMICET

And robbed of all that is real.
Wealth is not worth, but values shared by all.
Safety is gained when no shelter is needed.
Beauty and grace are not physical traits,
but deep affectations that all can see.

CORELEAY

Her granddad Solaren had wealth, safety, grace and
beauty.

DOMICET

You knew nothing of Solaren.

CORELEAY

(curt)

I married his son. I ought to know my father.

DOMICET

(contemplative)

You think you knew my brother? You have no sense.

I only knew him because… he was … my friend.
I spent my <u>life</u> with him, he spent his with me.
The truth is, I never met him until …
a few years before his death; then was his life.

In our teens all is lost to mystery.
In our family years one tries to survive;
Only then comes the calm of wisdom, freedom.
Only then is the true king born, who can rule.

I met him for a meal, the calm of the day.
We had our business, of course, and worked that out
first.
But then we still had time, to wait on others.
Our lives are consumed, if lucky, with helping.

      (pointing at the tapestry)

Like the burst of sun rays at the break of morn,
streaming forth to enlighten all within sight.
Our talks to and from opened the door wide,
to a new world of wonder for me, and he.

After that first chance of verbal intercourse,
he sought me out; I sought him every chance, too.

      (pause, to look at Coreleay, staring)

Don't leer at me that way! It was not of the flesh!
Ours was a marriage of the mind! Even so,
we spent physical time together too.

      (defensive)

That is the only way two people can talk!

      (back to contemplative)

And talk we did, lost to the rest of the world,
wherever we sat, drank, ate, felt, danced, sensed,
    slept.
And, he governed.

CORELEAY

(with contempt)

Your governing is confused with politics!
No one is fooled when the serpent is alive.
Only at death do we call our king "hero."
Solaren was king, was no more, is no more.

SCRIBE enters Stage Left, carrying
IYSOBEL.

DOMICET

So Izabella must do more, can do more.
Deny her the learning, deny her the truth,
and you deny her the destiny.
Solaren would counsel so, if he were here.

CORELEAY

(furious)

Solaren is not here.
The truth is not here.
I shall not be here…

(grabbing Iysobel from Scribe)

And Iysobel never shall be here!

CORELEAY with IYSOBEL exits Stage Left.

DOMICET

(pacing, shouts)

Scribe! Where are your pen and ink! Hurry!

(takes a seat on the Throne)

SCRIBE

(takes up paper and pen from table)

Yes, sir, I am ready.

DOMICET

(contemplative)

Politics is a sin,
of stupidity.
One starts in the ranks, and
never attains the goal.

SCRIBE

(confused, writes nothing)

What would you have me write?

DOMICET

I am but a living scar: <u>experience</u>.
Fire will scar the skin,
and tears will scar the heart.
I am but a conglomerate of failure, tangled tissue,
a conscious corpse still breathing.

SCRIBE

(pretends to write)

Yes, master, if you say so….

DOMICET

At least Solaren escaped through the grave.
What did we ever achieve? We gained nothing!
My life, our dreams, our work, vanished, all for
     naught.
Politics of the people, siren to the vain.
And all in vain.

In despair, the DOMICET exits Stage
Left.

SCRIBE pauses, not knowing whether to
leave, looks around, and seeing no one,
relaxes, puts his pen and paper down.

SCRIBE

And my life? Only a reflection of his.

For he is master, and I, loyal servant.
So, too, the politician who succeeds;
For to win, one must entertain the masses.

And he owns not himself, but is an actor.
An actor is simply a modeler of words,
wearing popular thought as others wear clothes.
Thus the people own the king; and demand it so.

The people fire the fraud while the king wins,
and revolt when it suits their waffling interest.

                    Scribe exits Stage Left.

          (CURTAIN)

ACT II: UNIFICATION

Scene 2: Mausoleum Graveyard

SETTING: Stage Right Rear, partially concealed
                        is a family crypt, a columned door, the
                        name "Orvilla" carved into the mantle.

                        Stage Center Rear are headstones in a
                        graveyard; Stage Left Front is a wide
                        tree trunk, enough to hide a man. It
                        is dusk, long shadows marking the day.

AT RISE: ARTEMIS enters Stage Right, cautiously
                        looking about, carrying three bags of
                        gold coins, which he lays down at the
                        Mausoleum entryway. A stone sits aside
                        the gold. Artemis stands Center Rear
                        Stage, faces Stage Right toward the
                        crypt, hands clasped together.

                                ARTEMIS

        Dear father,
        Why did you burden me with first of line?
        Why must I struggle to maintain what's mine?
        I learned at your knee, of trade, of life,
        but never you threatened a world of strife.

        I lead no army; I wield no sword.
        The merchant's battlefield is all I know.
        Almaden's people are familiar to me,
        But how might I gain them to follow?

        A success in banking, a failure at court.
        A family I breed, and contempt for the sort
        of pandering it takes to sit on the throne.
        Take off this golden yoke! Leave me alone!

        It is your third son, the priest,
        who enjoys a passion to rule.
        His quality matters not the least,
        Try he fails, I am no fool.

                        CEPHAS enters Stage Left, to encounter
                        Artemis.

                                CEPHAS

Artemis! Might we speak?

                    ARTEMIS

                  (startled)

Oh! For <u>you</u>, I give all my time in this world.

                    CEPHAS

                  (pondering)

Time. Time.

Time is all-present, a sense perception.
We move from Touch, Taste, Smell, See, and Hear,
then repeat.
A life of sensation, for better or worse;
Then in explosion, or a whimper, we die.

                    ARTEMIS

While mankind progresses to victory,
conquering the giants,
slaying the dragons,
winning each day.
Let's not devalue human achievement!

                    CEPHAS

A ghost, a fake; the main are non-believers.
Do not blame the poor who cannot eat progress.

                    ARTEMIS

My only judge is my heart inside, not else.
Each morn I wake to try again; the people hang!
They own no claim on me; I own <u>my</u> soul.
And if I win, they win! I am no island!

                    CEPHAS

Fine for you, but… my own success needs… cash, power,
people.

ARTEMIS

(feigned, facetious)

Shock! Awe!

My ears go deaf from the lie!
Throughout the realm, a priest abandons all.
Yet to the world <u>you</u> now disclose your tie?
For sensory goods? Let not this angel fall!

CEPHAS

Cash, power, people, the tripod of life.
You think I disavow the essence of all?
Please, my brother, your shallowness is a knife.
Divorce all ties, then above I stand tall.

ARTEMIS

So, you need no cash?

CEPHAS

I would not touch cash, but… for the needy.
Money is a resource; I am the mule.

ARTEMIS

Your logic is an ass….

(smirks)

CEPHAS

Make your jokes, but do not deny the poor.
They need the food; your soul hangs in the balance.

ARTEMIS

Then cash you shall have!

                    ARTEMIS picks up a bag of coins and
                    tosses it to CEPHAS, who catches bag of
                    coins.

                              CEPHAS

Thank you, my brother.

                              ARTEMIS

So, you need no power?

                              CEPHAS

The flame of a candle can burn a village.
The smallest of effort can ignite a change.
A leader harnesses, small things grow large.
Soon they gain faith, and build a cathedral.

                              ARTEMIS

Your goal be nothing less than the House of God!
And you to preside, of course…

                              CEPHAS

                    (bows)

Only at the altar, to serve.

                              ARTEMIS

An altar to sacrifice.
Be sure it is <u>your</u> blood,
or that of a goat,
and not of the poor!

                              CEPHAS

I assure you, no midnight mass.

                              ARTEMIS

Then masons you shall have!

                         (picks up a stone and tosses it to
                         Cephas)

                              CEPHAS

                    (catches stone)

Thank you, my brother.

ARTEMIS

So, you need no people?

CEPHAS

Need? I need nothing but the faith in our God.

ARTEMIS

Need you no one to watch?
No one to pray?
No one to save?
No one to… pay?

CEPHAS

You mean tithe?
That is their gift as they choose, if they choose.

ARTEMIS

No one to confess?
No one to genuflect?

CEPHAS

The Church offers sanctity in many ways.

            (emotionally ecstatic)

Let the people choose;
Let the people rule;
Let the people come!

            (bows down on his knees, hands clasped
            in prayer)

ARTEMIS

Ah! To rule!
That is the nut, the core, the essence of your heart!
Third son, excluded; no scepter, no Throne.
So now the same but in your own realm.

CEPHAS

I am wounded amiss, no justice in this!

TALUS

(off-stage)

Hail Artemis!

CEPHAS pretends to exit Stage Left, but ducks in behind the trunk of the tree, waits and watches.

Enter TALUS Stage Right; ARTEMIS turns to meet him.

ARTEMIS

My blood lives in Talus!

(embrace)

TALUS

And mine in you!
Where flows Brother Cephas in our trilogy?

ARTEMIS

(discouraged)

A loose leaf, afloat alone,
He is possessed by designs of his own.
Rule from a church, rule from the Throne,
rule from any perch is his tone.

TALUS

That is false, I know.
For his intent is true,
that the three of us
should rule through you!

ARTEMIS

Yes, the world knows,
As first-son I reign,
and am reined;
As a horse with a bit,
for my life restrained.

(resists angrily)

I do not plan to follow blind fate.
I shall not be slave to my people or to my state!

                    TALUS

Calm, my brother.
Without you, Cephas nor I would be nothing.
Together, we own, the cash, the power, the people.
What better result than we share the scepter?

                         ARTEMIS reaches for the remaining 2
                         bags of gold, gives to Talus.

                    ARTEMIS

Here is your gold.
Hold onto your power!
I owe you one bag, your Brother in need.
As for Cephas,… trust not the people.

                    TALUS

You… refuse?

                    ARTEMIS

I decline the Throne.
I know not your power.
If the people's heart rests in your hands,
I yield to you.

                    (bows)

                    TALUS

It is not morals, but a practical concern.
We have the might, the command of plenty,
We have the people at every turn. Yet,
neither Cephas nor I have the money.

                    ARTEMIS

Then get a job.

                    (walks away)

TALUS

Work with us, brother:
A triumvirate, a team, a three-legged Throne.
We meet our goal as one, for no man stands alone.
The world may turn on a single axis,
But an economy grows not on taxes.

ARTEMIS

I am a merchant, no more.
I am cursed as first-son.
If you love me, leave me
to my work.

>   ARTEMIS Embraces Talus, then exits
>   Stage Right.
>
>   TALUS stands Center Rear Stage, faces
>   Stage Right toward the crypt, kneels on
>   one knee, clasps hands.

TALUS

Our father,
Why did you bestow one brother with gold,
The other a siren to sing to our nation?
And I?
The blood thirsty scythe, to balance accounts.
The man to make peace, through talk or by death.

What chance have I to entice the two others?
One who buys my hand on the cheap,
One who twists his words about my brain.
I am lost! Show me a simple path!

For what I desire is love, an embrace.
That they respect my place, and join in arms,
not sword, but flesh. To rule in one place
all three, whose passion our state warms.

Grant me this wish: cleanse my sins, wash my hand
of the truth in my reputation.
Give to me the chance that I rule the land
A place of peace, a wealthy nation.

Enter CEPHAS from behind the tree trunk
Stage Left, surprising Talus.

CEPHAS

Artemis fights the natural law,
That power and money control the people.

TALUS

To an extent, you are correct. A dice roll.

CEPHAS:

The air, the water, the soil, the fire, these are
    certain.
Does ruling the people not follow the law?

TALUS

The mind of the people follows no law.
They fear death and the sword, and suppress their
    will.
But offer them hope, an eagle's claw.
No money, no power, they opt to kill.

CEPHAS

I tire of theory; our Artemis is weak.
He has no vision, no will.
He leaves us with no choice:
to kill or be killed.

TALUS

Stop! You rant, you rave!
Fratricide, regicide, suicide!
You forget all Artemis gave.
Without him, we kill our country.

CEPHAS

(dismissive)

Mindless pawn.
Artemis stands in our way,
for you are… second son.
When Artemis goes,

Talus arrives.

                    TALUS

So much for a triumvirate;
now talk a duo.
But why would I share?
What value do you add?

                    CEPHAS

You have the power;
I have the people.
Where is the money?
We must work together.

                    TALUS

I am no merchant;
I am no priest.
You fill one post,
what of the other?

                    CEPHAS

Money is water, filling in holes.
We will join forces, meeting those goals.
Take care of your brother, our partnership shows,
money will yield to what everyone knows.

                    TALUS

For a man of the cloth, you are of stone.

                    CEPHAS

For a man of God, I am a rock.

                    TALUS

Our will be done.

                    CEPHAS

Our will be done.

                    Both embrace.

Exit TALUS, Stage Left.

CEPHAS stands Center Rear Stage, faces
Stage Right toward the crypt, kneels on
both knees, hands clasped in prayer.

CEPHAS

My father,
Why did you reject this son of your flesh?
Abandoned to church, an alien pack?
My mother away, my brothers enmeshed
in my home, with the love that I lack?

And now we debate, to join or to fight.
Your destiny vague, your doing by lack
of attention to your third son. Do not deny!
I am the proof. While you lived, apparent success.

But in death, I am the truth. Crisis at hand.
So send me a sign, that I may take charge.
To lead both my brothers, and I rule the land.
United our hearts, the sum to enlarge.

And now, you lie as dust in an ancient grave.
But I thrive! Among the natural forces.
I help, I care, I strive to succeed, save
The lack of my brothers' resources.

CEPHAS stands, grasps his hands, bows,
and exits Stage Right.

(CURTAIN)

ACT II: UNIFICATION

Scene 3: The Throne Room, Fortress Centrale

SETTING: Interior of the Throne Room, Banquet
                            Table Center Stage Front, set for
                            dinner.

AT RISE: The DOMICET sits on his stool Stage
                            Right, thinking. TALUS slowly circles
                            the Throne, touching and feeling it, as
                            though sizing it. CEPHAS sits at table
                            sipping wine. Enter ARTEMIS Stage Left,
                            striding. Enter CORELEAY following
                            Artemis, smiling, both sit to eat.

                    ARTEMIS

News my dear uncle!
A caravan comes!
Business for the town, opportunity!
All of us gain when appears a shiny coin!

                    DOMICET

          (despondent)

Your coin slows your brothers from their goal;
Only a postponement, only a delay.

                    ARTEMIS

Always the same, always the same.
I do not care for the power, for the people.
A distraction, a diversion.
Let me profit!

                    DOMICET

First son, will you not rule?

                    ARTEMIS

          (hesitates, respectful)

I will… not rule.

(sits and eats)

CORELEAY

And with a sated stomach,
His tongue soaked with spirits,
Blind to our nation's future,
Iysobel he disinherits!

DOMICET

(ignoring the controversy, stands)

The banquet! Yes!
Surrender one's duty,
Give into the physical needs.
The stomach rules the mind.

CORELEAY throws her hands up in
disgust, starts eating.

TALUS

Then I am second son.
I have the power,
all I lack is purse…
and love.

DOMICET

A purse is like a magnet; it follows success.
Yet Artemis repels.

TALUS

Then I shall be gravity!
The people love a victory,
love a general, love a soldier, love a winner.
Let the apples fall in my orchard,
Let the merchant's cash come my way!

DOMICET

Love? For you? Or love for others?
Start with your neighbors, then look to their mothers.
Why would you ask us to call you a lord,
other than those you pay… for a sword?

TALUS

Vile stain! That I suffer from fighting a war.[8]
My record unblemished, in serving the state.
Now that the politics seep in the door,
I must defend, against contentment and hate.

They sat at their hearths, content while we fought,
To protect home and life. And when we return,
The success they expected by the coin that they
bought,
Our lives are nothing, once of victory they learn.

So veterans march through our streets of peace.
A polite applause, a smile from their beaus.
A chest of medals, a scar, a house to lease.
But a home? The truth a Soldier knows.

So here I stand, the second son,
Not willing to go, nor fade in the past.
The power I have, the money I won.
The people accept the die that they cast!

                    Domicet walks to Talus, kisses his
                    forehead.

                    TALUS

                    (drops to his knees)

Do you love me?

                    DOMICET

Of course, my son, I love you.

                    (both embrace)

To love is to care. Your past we forgive.
And forgiveness is Love. No consequence.
The reverse is indifference. Even hate is love.
Fear only that we care nothing for you.

For when we forget, your legacy is dead.
Your honor, so nobly won, escapes with time.
My hope? That your love for your <u>brothers</u> prevails.

---

[8] The Veterans' Soliloquy.

Of course, my son, I love you.

> (embrace again)

CEPHAS

And what of me? Do you love me too?

DOMICET

I love you too!

> The DOMICET walks to Cephas, kisses his
> forehead, mechanically, turns away.

TALUS

But you do not trust him. He calculates in the dark.

> (sits to eat)

CEPHAS

Am I honored, or insulted?

TALUS

An honor all will know, as all can share.
One knows an insult from its essential truth.

> (returns to eating)

ARTEMIS

Cephas is the smart one.
Cephas is the book.
A record of us all, an account to reckon.
Whether debit or credit, is in his look!

CEPHAS

Am I honored, or insulted?

ARTEMIS

I'll not judge you; judge yourself.

> (returns to eating)

DOMICET

Stop this now.
Eat your dinner,
savor your friendship.
Affirm your brotherhood.

ARTEMIS

I eat, therefore I am.
First I see what is to become me.

(looks at fork of food)

My ears hear my friends, happy to join the meal.
The smell invites us to dine, I taste the wine. (sips)
I feel alive, no power, no people.
To live, the conflict must be ignored.

(returns to eating)

DOMICET

If the conflict is past, you died a quiet death.
Many a buried soldier might agree,
if they had the lips to taste, and to talk;
To choose a scent, or to hear a verse:
They, too, would feel alive.

But they died. Let them rest. They are no more.
Brother Cephas asks for more, to build his fame.

CEPHAS

Am I honored, or insulted?

CORELEAY

(angry, insistent)

You three must <u>stop</u>, at odds, each strong while each
     weak.
Yet to rule, you must unite, you must seek peace!

CEPHAS

(stands from meal)

These hallowed halls do speak of the fame.
Collective dead, we hear shouts as they claim,
That man not waste life on a taste or a smell,
Nor watch as others debate to their hell.

But seek to validate their lives in deeds,
Not cast to fortune an idle fate.
To feel alive from their wants and needs,
Solaren kept trying 'til the day he fell.

But…he failed.

(sits, resumes eating)

DOMICET

(glances at Cephas)

You did not know him as he sought success.

Do you think my brother was wise when he was young?
Did all who saw him listen to his tongue?
No, just like any boy, Solaren was vain;
Physique over mind, all brawn and no brain.

A leader must learn to persuade other men,
who choose to follow and together gain;
Or, without looking back, "Slay!" they advise.

(pauses, remembering)

Recall your scripture, Solomon the wise?
Among the ambitious, the killer is King.

CORELEAY

(stands)

You selfish siblings! Strut to divide the land,
Think only of funds, of power, of might.
The heir is Iysobel, a queen with your hand,
Give your sword, cite your law; a reign of right!

CEPHAS

It is more complex than she;
What is in that, for me?

TALUS

Of the soldiers she'll command
First my allegiance they'll demand.

ARTEMIS

The power today is only the coin.
She rules only once the merchants will join.

                    CORELEAY stands, circles table, wine in
                    hand, looking at each in turn.

CORELEAY

What is it that each you want? Your heart's desire?

CEPHAS

I shall say: To be loved! To be loved by all!

CORELEAY

You mean adored?

CEPHAS

Yes… Why not!

They kneel at my altar, they kiss my hand.
I am known, I am loved, throughout this land.
Let me be sainted, that none my life forget.
My name, my face, adored by all, each eye wet!

CORELEAY

Then I grant you this, Brother Cephas! Your life
to be adored by all, in all, through all time.
Your graven image in homes and on altars,
Golden Baal on fire never shone so brightly!

But what shall you pay? For here is the price:

You must be martyred, by those you love.
Your fame breeds envy, they suspect a fraud.
Your own people, know not what they do
But too late. Thereafter, you shall be ADORED.

                    CEPHAS

                    (laughs with contempt)

A Judas kiss is what you say?

                    (shrugs)

At least, I am loved.

                    (returns to eating)

                    CORELEAY continues walking around the
                    table.

                    CORELEAY

And what of you, dear Talus? What is your heart's
desire?

                    TALUS

Power, of course. Military might!
The fruits of victory, conqueror of all.
To stand on the hill viewing Almaden,
And know that all I see, all I hold, I rule.

                    CORELEAY

Then I grant you this, General Talus,
The conqueror of us, the people, the land.
Not a step be walked, not a word be said
That does not reckon Talus as compass.

But what shall you pay? For this is not free,

Yet slavery.
They do not forget, they do not forgive;
Those you suppress shall keep account.
 A mark of hate, for every life lost,

On a field of red death, you shall have POWER!

                        TALUS

                (laughs with contempt)

At least, I rule.

                (shrugs)

I can live with that.

                (returns to eating)

                CORELEAY continues walking around the
                table.

                        CORELEAY

Artemis, my dearest? What is your heart's desire?

                        ARTEMIS

Why, all the gold in the world! To no end.
To control all commerce, to build great cities.
That I may, that <u>we</u> may, travel the seas,
To do good works, to possess all I wish!

                        CORELEAY

                (sadly)

Then I grant you this, my love,
The gold you shall have! All that passes in the land.
Invade each trade route, shackle each banker's hand…

Or be the bank!
Finance the trade, the wars, the kingdoms.

But what shall you pay? Forfeit all else, and,

Your family. For gold, you lose all time
To smell the flowers, to see the art,
To hear the music, to taste the bread, …

Or to feel the press of your wife's breast!
Alone on your death bed, yet you shall have GOLD!

                    ARTEMIS

                  (head down)

I work for all of us.

                  (shrugs)

No one thanks me.

                  (returns to eating)

            CORELEAY continues walking around.

                  CORELEAY

Cyril, Domicet Emeritus? What is your heart's desire?

                  DOMICET

Why, more time, of course! Each aged man
Comes to a point where he foresees the end.
And shakes in fear that he has failed, but for
One more chance!   To balance the books, to make
amends.

            CORELEAY walks to Cyril, takes off his
            hat and kisses his head.

                  CORELEAY

Alas my dear uncle, this I cannot give.
Long have you lived; what account must you fix?
No one else rules; change what you like!
Today is your day, and tomorrow; just live!

And what shall you pay? Why, nothing! You are paid!

Your life's account is balanced each waking day.
Sit outside, taste of life! Hear the stories.
Embrace your friends.
Tomorrow, forever, you shall have PEACE.

DOMICET

(sits back, contemplates)

Yet I have one more task before I pass.

> CORELEAY sits at the table next to Artemis and eats.

CEPHAS

Is it love or adoration you need before you pass?

DOMICET

Neither love nor adoration need I from you.

> TALUS reaches for a bowl of food on the table.

TALUS

Pass the power; you forfeit it by idleness.

DOMICET

You have no idea the power I possess.

ARTEMIS

Let me pay for a trip, to ease your mind.

DOMICET

(stands, points in turn to each son)

Rue the day you did not join,
A congress to preserve this nation.
Each in turn, you might rule,
Or earn life's condemnation.

CORELEAY

(stands, walks around the room with wine glass)

I am just a woman, as is my girl.

But just is her cause. In blindness, risk your life.
For no force can stop that blind rage will hurl
When those people you press enter the strife.

I seal with this curse: your <u>neck</u> at risk!
You shall die, I shall die, your hour thus ends.
And Iysobel ascends, so peace descends,
Our land to love, to grow, the power shifts!

                CORELEAY throws her wine glass to the
                floor, shattering, exits Stage Left.

                (CURTAIN)

ACT III: RESOLUTION

Scene 1: The Courtyard, Merchant's Home

SETTING: Ibid, Act I, Scene Three.

AT RISE: ARTEMIS is at his desk working,
                        CORELEAY sitting on the center bench
                        facing away, reading a book.

                        CORELEAY

    Your brothers weigh on my mind. We are at risk.

                        ARTEMIS

    No, I pay them well.
    Cephas gave me terms.
    I gave him cash, and
    Talus stays the course.

                        CORELEAY

    It is Iysobel of whom I worry.
    Uncles in name, neither in faith.

                        ARTEMIS

    Would they not tell me so?
    Would they not show their hands?

    Cephas calculates, for sure;
    But Talus keeps no secrets.
    While Cephas slinks through darkened halls,
    Talus bellows, bludgeons, bleeds, and bows
    To the walls of reality.

                        CORELEAY

    You are right, always right, when thought prevails.
    But these times are not the norm; we are at risk,
    That conflict prevails, and blinds men's reason.
    Do not trust even your kin, the Throne at stake.

ARTEMIS

(stops work, looks to Coreleay)

For sure the times are not the norm.
Yet each day begins, and each night closes.
The ships set sail, the carts do roll, and I
know nothing else.
I fear, but do my best.

CORELEAY

Then love me, and share my fear.

ARTEMIS

I do love you.

Enter TALUS and CHARLES.

TALUS

Good day, dear brother Artemis!

ARTEMIS

And to you, Talus!
Welcome, Charles. (aside) The obedient cur!

(turns back to his work)

CORELEAY

An hospitable visit might be the brother alone.
The duo is to some purpose.

TALUS

My purpose is power, not for me, but for our brother.
Your welfare, our unity, the state's future,
Together to rule, together as one.
Our father lives on through our generation.

CHARLES

(pulls out Cephas' rope belt to show)

Cephas sends proof of his sincerity.

A tie that binds, not a robe but a Throne.
A tri-footed stool where all shall sit,
Strength at each others' back, not weakness alone.

ARTEMIS

I have aided Cephas in all he asks.
If he asks no more, why do you?
It is your fortune to share your share with him.
Or, is it my fortune that, you seek my fortune?

TALUS

Thank you for your fortune, and my fortune in share.
You leave us at loss, to decline the chair.
Can our fate, two brothers left to rule be fair?
While your accounts leave our estates bare.

CORELEAY

(puts book down)

Send them away, Artemis!
Bare blackmail, to my ears.

(goes back to her book)

ARTEMIS

A futile gesture, to treat with habit,
As a mongrel returns when time for a meal.

CORELEAY

(stands)

There is but one solution to their baying,
They demand to be governed, or govern.
The lack of decision is the culprit;
So rise to the chance! Who knows the future?

But know this:

Time fills the void, abides no control.
Time creeps on, or rushes in. Either way,
We ride the wind of time; we control little.

Best we embrace chance when favored, when good.

           (returns to the bench, back to Artemis)

ARTEMIS

I tire this repeat, the bang of a drum.
Hear now my words:

Time may choose our destiny,
but it is not my time.
How many times must I decline?
Know my heart!

           ARTEMIS gets up from desk with book,
           goes to center bench, and sits back-to-
           back with Coreleay, to read.

TALUS

Yet now is the time! The people await!
Outside your home, that you pronounce,
the resolution of our quandary.

           (kneels before Artemis)

And Cephas awaits, outside your door,
for a sign of acceptance, your blessing of our cause.
Embrace your brother!

ARTEMIS

I curse my brother!
He begs, I give;
He plots, he plans!
His grasp knows no end!

If he has the people, then let him lead!
If you have the power, then do your deed!

TALUS

           (stands)

So be it, brother, that we break apart.
This is not my choice. Severance shall break our

        heart.
But progress demands resolution today.
The step we take now offers no retreat.   Please join
        us….

                    ARTEMIS

            (without looking up)

Never.

                    TALUS

Then your doing….

                    TALUS signals to CHARLES, who using
                    Cephas' rope belt strangles Artemis and
                    Coreleay, back-to-back. Dropping their
                    books, ARTEMIS and CORELEAY grasp at
                    their necks, then succumb together.

                    CHARLES steps back. TALUS walks to the
                    dead couple, re-arranges the rope belt
                    so that each end hangs over them in
                    front, like a decorative necklace.

                    TALUS

In life they dressed in exquisite clothes.
In death, they wear an exquisite pose.
In life bound by marriage,
In death bound by rope.
Their love not disparaged,
Their fate is our hope!

                    TALUS stands back to admire the scene,
                    then exits Stage Right, picking up a
                    bag of coin off Artemis' desk as he
                    walks by.

                    Talus gone, CHARLES walks to Stage
                    Left, then shouts:

                    CHARLES

Alarm! Alarm!

                    CHARLES rushes out Stage Right.

                    CEPHAS rushes in from Stage Left, stops
                    in shock at the scene.

                              CEPHAS

Oh! Heavenly mandate, must this be their fate?
Efforts to share, now all come too late.
Can this be the crop of the seeds of dissent?
Our plans were but words, now formed into deeds.
I sought to share, but not in this.
My belt to bind, now empty the chair.

                    Cephas paces frantically.

It cannot be, was I so blind? That I missed
my brothers' cause.
How dare he advance, without me!
I shall wait him out, cut the deal, still prevail;
Or cut my throat and join the elders,
No point to proceed. Talus has won.

                    VILLAGERS rush in from Stage Left.

                              CEPHAS

Behold! The tragedy of our age!

                           VILLAGER ONE

Behold the rope! It does appear as Cephas' belt.

                           VILLAGER TWO

                      (looking at Cephas)

Oh, Brother, your waist is accusingly bare.

                          VILLAGER THREE

An asp has no waist, and thus needs no belt.

CEPHAS

(praying, eyes upward)

Do your eyes deceive you? It is the violence of Talus
It is the hand of Charles Calay!
I gave them my rope, my belt, in trust!
Dear Lord, forgive them, for they know not what they
do!

CEPHAS backs away from Villagers.

VILLAGER THREE

A sure proof will be we know how to do,
if hanging from rope, you're alive or dead!

(all laugh)

VILLAGER ONE

We'll hold a trial! We'll need a jury!

VILLAGER TWO

We've no time before church service calls.

VILLAGER THREE

To church? You return the groundhog to his hole.

CEPHAS

Hold your hand! Move no further!

You lost your king, and now his eldest.
What more tragedy might you invite, to wreck the ship
     of state?
Tie yourself to the mast, for still the storm rages!
And in calmer waters, seek your leader.

VILLAGER ONE

It is not raining…

VILLAGER TWO

Yes, where is Talus?

VILLAGER THREE

To our duty!

                VILLAGERS grab CEPHAS who struggles,
                and all exit Stage Left.

                (CURTAIN)

ACT III: RESOLUTION

Scene 2: Finale, The Throne Room, Fortress Centrale

SETTING: Ibid, Act I, Scene One.

AT RISE: The DOMICET sits on the small stool
                              Stage Right beneath the window, with
                              his back to TALUS, Stage Center.

                              Offstage, sound over of military drums,
                              drumroll, then single bass drum beat.

                              The DOMICET buries his head in his
                              hands.

                              TALUS

It is done. Fate has taken my Brother Cephas.

                              DOMICET

What fate prevails not planned by men?
I have lived too long, too long to blame a ghost.
First Solaren, then Artemis, now Cephas.
No fate aims Death's scythe so well.

                              TALUS

Surely you cannot prove blame.
The good of the state does not await.

                              DOMICET

Cephas stood here to tell that I should rule. No?

                              TALUS

Your age but delays the true choice.
The good of the state does not await.

                              DOMICET

Cephas asked to share the Throne, all three to rule.
No?

TALUS

Artemis paid, but then declined.
The good of the state does not await.

> The DOMICET stands, confronts Talus
> near the Throne.

DOMICET

The cock crows thrice!
Deny the royal lineage?

TALUS

I am the eldest son.
This cannot be denied.

DOMICET

Yet the heir of the eldest son still lives.

TALUS

An infant!

DOMICET

Forget the line, do you claim:
The money, the power, the heart of the people?

TALUS

The money arrives, like the sun, like the wind,
with each caravan, timely, always, but a job for a
    clerk.

DOMICET

And the power?

TALUS

I led our armies even for Solaren!
I lead, I fight, I _am_ the power!

DOMICET

And… the heart of the people?

TALUS

As you love me, they shall love me.
In time, as a youthful bride, they shall learn
the precious price of peace.
I shall persuade with a coin as needed, or… else they
    die.
What choice do they have… but to love me?

DOMICET

And what of your niece?

TALUS

Ah! Iysobel shall adorn our realm!
She is the key to their hearts.
Do not doubt, dear Domicet, the value of the child.
She shall lead the parade, her feature on our coin,
her voice to plead our case!
She is true royalty, and I shall treat her so.
But I shall rule.

DOMICET

And when she comes of age?
When she sees your true self?
What then, Talus,
when the people love her more than you?

TALUS

It shall never be so.

DOMICET

It is inevitable.

TALUS

Then inevitably… she shall die.

> The DOMICET quietly picks up the knife
> from the side table, whirls around and
> stabs Talus in the abdomen. Shocked,
> TALUS holds onto the Domicet's arms.

                        TALUS

But, Uncle, I thought you loved me!

                        DOMICET

I did,

                    (thrusts knife again)

and I DO!

                    TALUS collapses to floor, dead.

                        DOMICET

A fruit tree flowers, its blooms become fruit,
fragrant and pretty, such are our children.
But, leave them on the tree, they shrivel and drop.
Corrupt in their life, they rot on the ground.

                    The DOMICET walks calmly to Rear Stage
                    Center, rips down the red curtain, and
                    covers the dead body of Talus.

And now, my Talus, you'll rot <u>in</u> the ground.

                    (pacing, shouts to Stage Left)

Scribe! Come in here! Hurry!

                    The DOMICET cautiously takes a seat at
                    the edge of the Throne chair.

                    SCRIBE enters from Stage Left, paper
                    and pen in hand; taken aback at the
                    heap on the floor, then composes
                    himself, picks up pen and paper.

                        SCRIBE

Yes, sir, I am ready.

                        DOMICET

Draft a death warrant, for the arrest of Charles
     Calay.
Sign it, "Cyril Orvilla, Domicet,"
<u>not</u> Emeritus, "of Almadon".

In my own right, patient, but overdue.

                    SCRIBE

Your will be done.
Do you need me further?

                    DOMICET

                (contemplative)

Oh, yes, I have just begun.

We must arrange things, plan for the future,
Balance accounts, deed the land, pay our debts.
Order must be brought to a normal course,
Things - made - right.

                (pauses, stands)

Earthquakes shift rivers, where was no water;
Brush fires burn grass black, to enrich the soil;
Nature's provision disrupts for reason.
Things upset, now right, all in their season.

My brother was king, holding all power.
Wealthy soldier he, won people's honor.
His death split in three the power before.
No person could own this chair evermore.

Three sons to follow:

                    SCRIBE

First, Artemis.

                (raises one finger)

                    DOMICET

My nephew and niece, possessed wealth and fame,
Much fortune, much luck, but no common sense.
What good was the gold? A metal so cold
That one's heart could freeze, and love nothing else.

All others, they worked that gold was produced
In bags, in wallets, they kept in a box.

Now they own naught but the seed, my dear girl.
So we must sow that, (stands), in her time, she reaps!

(sits on the stool, contemplating)

SCRIBE

Second, Talus:

(raises two fingers)

DOMICET

My warlike nephew knew how to destroy.
No goal, no moral, other than to kill.
Do not mistake me: he too had his place.
A purse freely gained to purchase a death.

He sought pure power, elusive elixir,
Corrupting his heart, scarring his pure skin,
Until no longer recognizable, died. (jumps up)
Not by my hand! Note that, scribe!

(points to Talus)

By <u>his</u> hand, alone!

Now, to put the pieces together again,
To function, a home, a family too.
Unity of purpose, a single soul,
Again a city, for all, a goal!

Money to buy our military might.
Soldiers to keep law, enforce people's choice.
People to their work, earn the common wealth.
There is restored the Triangle of Peace!

SCRIBE

Third, Cephas:

(raises three fingers)

DOMICET

My priestly nephew, oh! My heart is so sad!
Such good intent to heal this savage world.

Yes, that was their will; he earned and owned it!
Then threw it away, sold priceless for gold.

Those clerical robes were just a disguise
By which first he stole, then judged, plotted,
    planned.
Earned each person's trust, then only to breach,
To use every soul as with rusted tools.

Now he too is gone, by the People's Will.
He earned the gallows of his own free choice.
Obstinate, his own ignorance;
No matter the cause, the fate is the same, black
    verdict: death.

SCRIBE

(stops writing, interrupts)

But my honor, that is the past. Of what future would
you have me write?

DOMICET

(resolute)

Take this down! I act but as a trustee,
No right, no power, no money, no office of my own.
We therefore bequeath, (pauses thinking),
The land, the vines, the manse, the whole –
The money is hers, we only confirm.

With gold we buy the soldiers to command.
They a fickle lot, pleased to serve the coin,
To keep the peace of common will.
A task made simple by such innate strength and charm.

The people will buy, and, the people will sell.
More money will flow, from pocket to purse,
To soldier, to man, to merchant, and again.
The lubricant of happiness becomes – wealth!

Days of my brother, days of unity,
Once more shall visit, this land, by my hand.
Money, might, the will, people together,
Centered on the NAME, a beautiful One!

SCRIBE:

(confused)

And what <u>name</u>, would you have me sign?

> Enter IYSOBEL, Stage Left, climbs onto
> Throne; DOMICET grins.

DOMICET

The name IS… a-BELLA!

(CURTAIN)

-- 30 --